CONQUERORS
IN THE
MAKING

Life—the Great Adventure

CYNTHIA LEPORI

WESTBOW
P R E S S®
A DIVISION OF THOMAS NELSON
& ZONDERVAN

All Scripture quotations, unless otherwise indicated, are taken from the Holy
Bible, New International Version®, NIV®. Copyright ©1973, 1978, 1984, 2011 by
Biblica, Inc.™ Used by permission of Zondervan. All rights reserved worldwide.
www.zondervan.com The "NIV" and "New International Version" are trademarks
registered in the United States Patent and Trademark Office by Biblica, Inc.™

WestBow Press books may be ordered through booksellers or by contacting:

WestBow Press
A Division of Thomas Nelson & Zondervan
1663 Liberty Drive
Bloomington, IN 47403
www.westbowpress.com
1 (866) 928-1240

ISBN: 978-1-9736-4898-7 (sc)
ISBN: 978-1-9736-4900-7 (hc)
ISBN: 978-1-9736-4899-4 (e)

Library of Congress Control Number: 2018914848

Print information available on the last page.

WestBow Press rev. date: 03/05/2019

"I press on to take hold of that for which
Christ Jesus took hold of me."

Philippians 3:12

DEDICATIONS

This book is dedicated to my beautiful mother and sisters. As a close-knit family, we've had wonderful times together. We have also survived some extremely hard trials. Through love and forgiveness, we have stuck together through it all.

I also dedicate it to people facing seemingly impossible challenges who need to know that they can conquer any feat if Jesus is their source of strength.

CONTENTS

PREFACE

Life ~ what a trip!

I have come to the conclusion that an interesting way to look at life is to see it as an ever-growing collection of opportunities and challenges. When combined, they can be seen as an adventure — an exciting adventure.

Our lives include what I call "interesting" experiences which God uses to build our characters and make us who we are. We do not always understand His ways. Most of us rarely do.

I have been a Christian who has encountered enough situations which I have not chosen to experience that I've learned not to stress out when they occur. Well... I should say that I am learning not to stress out. It is through those situations that God has taught me—and is continually teaching me—to be a person determined to overcome my challenges. I know that the only way I can overcome is by trusting God to enable me to come out on top.

This book is the result of my desire to encourage others

to believe they can be victorious through all circumstances if they have accepted Jesus as their Savior because Jesus can take them to places they cannot reach by their own efforts.

It is natural for me to try to take the "steering wheel" of my life and try to move toward the places I want to be. But, since God's path for me has not always been my own, I've learned the importance of trusting Him in the positions He has placed me.

Romans 8:37 is one of my favorite scriptures. It says "No, in all these things we are more than conquerors through Him who loved us." I've learned that God will give us the strength and the wisdom to overcome our personal battles if we refuse to give up. God will make us stronger and more resilient as we trust Him.

Life truly is one big adventure! You never know what tomorrow will bring. If you are going through a difficult time, hang in there. It will end one day soon. If you're experiencing a blessing today, take advantage of the opportunity to enjoy each moment.

Not only can we trust that Jesus will enable us to win our current battles. We can trust Him to make us victorious in our future pursuits.

You can be confident that you are not only a conqueror. You are a conqueror in the making!

INTRODUCTION

Life is the greatest adventure you'll ever experience!

Peace that passes understanding is a gift—a gift that all of us desire. It is a blessing received only by people who know that all things will turn out well for them... even if they don't know how it will happen. The only faith or belief system that I know of which promises that is Christianity.

Joy is an internal strength which is evidenced by a spirit of exultation or peace... whether we are happy or unhappy. Joy is something you can't conjure up.

Jesus is my source of peace and joy. I know that without Him I would have neither of these. As my life progresses, I've continually learned the importance of that truth. Jesus is the only one who can enable us to relax from the pressures of life – at this moment — because we know we are where we are supposed to be — at this moment — even if it is not where we want to stay.

A Paradigm Shift

Life gets exciting when you begin to look at it through a different lens — a new paradigm. Instead of seeing your difficulties as hardships, you begin to see them as challenges that you must confront and overcome.

Many times, our challenges are simply incorrect ideas which need to be captured. The Bible says that our struggles are spiritual, not of this world. It says "though we live in the world, we do not wage war as the world does." The weapons we fight with are not the weapons of the world, but spiritual weapons — faith, prayer, the Word of God, and praise. Through the use of those weapons we can demolish arguments and every pretension that sets itself up against the knowledge of God. We must take captive every thought to make it obedient to Christ. (II Corinthians 10:3-5)

As Christians, we can face our challenges with the confidence of knowing that our God will bring us through each one victoriously. We can believe this because we serve a God who has promised victory to His children.

This book was written out of my desire to encourage others to face their challenges with grace while fighting spiritual battles that threaten to defeat them. I want to encourage others to believe that, through trusting Jesus with the cares of their lives, they can overcome any obstacles.

Like most people, my life has been one of challenges

and personal ups and downs. One thing is for sure — I have learned that I can have a constant peace and inner strength if I trust the Lord and put my confidence in Him.

God has shown me, time and time again, that life is a series of challenges which I can conquer if I trust Him to make me victorious in each of them. He is still teaching me to not be fearful because He will be there to catch me if I come close to falling.

The purpose of this book is to help you see yourself as a conqueror who can overcome any challenge. I wrote it to encourage you to trust that the Lord is cheering you on as you pursue your dreams and achievements that you didn't think were possible.

I hope it helps you realize that you are a warrior who has already won the war if you trust Jesus. I hope it helps you look at life as a great experience of victory which includes many chances to conquer your personal battles along the way. If we trust God and learn to confront our challenges correctly our challenges will no longer dictate our level of happiness.

The battles that we face can make us more resilient and able to walk in God's peace. We can rest in Christ's love, knowing that He will restore us.

God is getting you ready for a new adventure. He is preparing you for the next chapter of your story. It may include a few battles, but you will not be shaken if your faith is in Christ. He will enable you to be a conqueror.

I can do all this through Him who gives me strength.

—Philippians 4:13

I

YOU ARE A CONQUEROR

*In all things we are more than conquerors
through Him who loved us.*

—Romans 8:37

What does it take to be a conqueror? Obviously, there are
many answers to the question.

The first and most important requirement is having
something to conquer. That is where the story begins.

Your life is a story. It had a start. It will have a finish. It is
full of challenges and victories. No matter what experiences
you have had and what events are coming your way I can
assure you of one thing; your life will be an adventure — a
great adventure.

Adventure is defined as "an exciting or remarkable
experience" and "an undertaking usually involving danger
and unknown risks". Adventures can be exhilarating. They

can also be terrifying. Although some challenges can be interesting — even fun — the essence of the word indicates that they will require a lot of strength.

I don't know what events your life has been comprised of, but I feel confident in saying that you have had to confront many challenges. With the right perspectives, we can learn to see our challenges as experiences that make our lives positive adventures, especially as we learn to trust the Lord to help us conquer them.

Having Done All to Stand — Stand

We can take it for granted that we cannot avoid challenges. In facing my challenges, large and small, I've learned that standing on Scripture is critical to accomplish the victory I am seeking. One of the most impactful scriptures in my life is Romans 8:28.

> *And we know that in all things God works for the good of those who love Him, who have been called according to His purpose.*
>
> —Romans 8:28

As Christians, we can be overcomers. No matter what paths we may decide to take we will most likely face some resistance. But, fear not! Victory awaits us as we learn to call on God and trust Him to carry us through each fight.

The Choice is Yours

The sum of our life lessons serve to create tools that God uses to carve out our character and lead us on a path to a marvelous destination. The choices we encounter represent 'forks in the road' along the avenues upon which we travel. Our happiness is determined by how we respond to those choices.

The ultimate choice will always be 'How will I respond to this particular experience?' Our responses are critical to our futures.

Our answers to this question will result in either a positive or a negative outcome. Our trust in Jesus Christ and our decisions to make Him the Lord of our lives determine the ease in which we are able to handle our life events.

We can be confident of one thing — God is always on His children's side. He truly is. He will lead us into victory. Our role is to continue trusting Him. Keep moving forward and do not give up. He will make you a conqueror along the way!

Scriptures

"What, then shall we say in response to these things? If God is for us, who can be against us." Romans 8:31

"The LORD makes firm the steps of the one who delights in Him; though he may stumble, he will not fall, for the LORD upholds him with His hand." Psalm 37:23-24

Reflections

1. Do you see yourself as a conqueror? Why?

_____

_____

_____

   Why not?

_____

_____

_____

2. Name a few ways that you have triumphed in your life.

_____

_____

_____

3. Have you ever overcome a personal battle that meant so much to you that you feel the Lord allowed it just to show you the joy of victory?

Remember that victory.

Let it build your faith to face any challenges you may be confronting.

II

THE MIGHTY HAND OF GOD

With a mighty hand and an outstretched arm;
His love endures forever.

— Psalm 136:12

How many ways have you used the word "hand"? In today's English, it is used to describe much more than an extremely functional human limb consisting of a palm and five fingers. Some examples of its usage include: Let's give him a hand for that performance! Would you mind giving me a hand with that? Hand me that pen, would you? Is someone wearing your hand-me-downs? Or, as the Beatles sang it, "I want to hold your hand...".

Along with the rest of humanity, one of our largest challenges can occur when we attempt the process of learning how try to walk joyfully through difficult experiences. In 1997, I broke my leg as the result of an ice-skating fall at the

Houston Galleria. A few days after my leg was put in a cast it became extremely painful. When I returned to my doctor he reset it because he thought that would resolve my problem. Unfortunately, that was not the solution. Over several months I encountered serious complications. The length of my recovery, along with the level of pain I experienced, led me to question whether I would ever walk pain-free again. Ouch!

During my recovery, through times of Bible study and prayer, I continuously noticed scriptures about God's hand. As a result, I recognized the dynamic phenomenon of God's hand representing His power. I was continually encouraged and became confident of one thing — the hand of God is one powerful hand!

Throughout the Bible, the hand of God is used to represent His providence, His omnipotence, His provision, His protection, His security, and His love.

> *For the LORD is the great God; the great King above all gods. In His hand are the depths of the earth, and the mountain peaks belong to Him. The sea is His, for He made it, and His hands formed the dry land.*
>
> *— Psalm 95:3-5*

The Bible's representation of God's power, through His hand, clearly exhibits that He is not just a deity who sits up in Heaven indifferently watching the events occurring on earth. He is omnipotent, all-powerful, and boundless. He has providence over everything.

Psalm 136 tells us that God used His strong hand and outstretched arm to deliver Israel as He divided the Red Sea. Moses encouraged the Israelites — many times — to trust that God was in complete control.

The Lord told the Israelites not to fear, assuring them that He was by their side. Can you imagine how it would feel to have God personally whisper that message in your ear? I could handle it!

> *So, do not fear, for I am with you; do not be dismayed, for I am your God. I will strengthen you and help you; I will uphold you with my righteous right hand.*
>
> — Isaiah 41:10

The Bible declares that it is God's will for man to know His peace, even in the midst of difficult trials. One way we can know His peace is by understanding that everything concerning us lies safely in the palm of God's hand.

We can be confident that the problems we consider

9

overwhelming are no challenge for Him! Not only is the hand of God a refuge for His children, the Bible asserts that large institutions, admired authorities, and respected establishments of the world are miniscule in His Hand. Our Lord's foresight is so much greater than man's. The Bible asserts that God laughs at the wicked because He knows their day is coming. (Ps. 37:13)

At the height of his battles, King David wrote "Though the Lord is exalted, He looks kindly on the lowly, He sees them from afar. Though I walk in the midst of trouble, You preserve my life. You stretch out your hand against the anger of my foes; with your right hand you save me." (Psalm 138:6-7). In the next verse, David states his belief that the Lord would not forsake the works of His own hands.

> *The Lord will vindicate me; your love, Lord, endures forever—do not abandon the works of your hands.*
>
> —Psalm 138:8

God wants us to give our cares to Him. Even more, He wants us to leave them there, being confident that He will take care of them. He continually desires to show His children the love that is the very essence of His nature. He promises that He will never allow more pressures to be put upon us than we are able to bear (1 Corinthians 10:13).

Our roles, as His children, are to trust Him, submit to Him, and learn to accept His will for our lives. This includes accepting His appointments for our lives, even those that appear to be limitations. God's "blessings" for us are often beyond our understanding.

> *Oh, the depth of the riches of the wisdom and knowledge of God! How unsearchable His judgments, and His paths beyond tracing out!*
>
> —Romans 11:33

You can be confident of God's love for you. When you feel lost, the Hand of God will guide you. When you feel weak, His Hand will carry you. If you've been mistreated, His gentle Hand will comfort you. When you are hurting, the Hand of Jesus heals. And, if you feel overwhelmed, God's Hand will hold you up.

Be assured, you can trust the Lord with your concerns. Everything really is in His hands. Through the work of His hands, none of your problems are too big for Him to solve. With the stroke of His hand, seemingly impossible tasks are very possible for God to complete. None of your needs are too large for Him to meet. None of your dreams are too large for Him to fulfill!

You can be confident of one thing — it is wise to walk hand-in-hand with God!

Scriptures

"You know when I sit and when I rise; You perceive my thoughts from afar. You discern my going out and my lying down; You are familiar with all my ways. You hem me in behind and before, and You lay your hand upon me." Psalm 139:2-3, 5

"Your eyes saw my unformed body; all the days ordained for me were written in Your book before one of them came to be." Psalm 139:16

"For as high as the heavens are above the earth, so great is His love for those who fear Him;" Psalm 103:11

Reflections

1. Do you understand what it feels like to be deeply cared for by a God who holds your life in His hands?

If you do not, meditate on scripture and ask God to show you the level of His love for you.

_____

_____

_____

2. Do you feel that you are in the hands of a loving God and confident that He will never drop you?

If you do not, what would it take for you to increase to trust Him?

_____

_____

_____

3. How deeply do you believe that Jesus knows and cares for you? Why?

_____

_____

_____

III

THE RACE IS ON!

Do you not know that in a race all the runners run but only one gets the prize? Run in such a way as to get the prize.

—I Corinthians 9:24

Do you enjoy competition? Are you a runner? Are you a swimmer? Are you a biker? Well, do you have a heartbeat? Welcome to the human race!

An interesting way of envisioning our lives is by comparing them to a marathon that we are determined to win. Our challenges represent goals and objectives on the way to the finish line. These goals, which may create stresses and difficulties, also make our lives invigorating and exhilarating.

Throughout the Bible are passages that exhibit ongoing examples of how life is comparable to a race where man is challenged in all sorts of ways, yet he is victorious as he lives to please God. The requirements to win this race include stamina, perseverance, determination, and a great sense of humor. As we develop these character traits, the only critical action we must take is to trust Jesus Christ for the strength and direction that will take us through the next steps He has for us.

Depending on the specifics of what we are confronting, trusting in the Lord can be a challenge. Many times, we are challenged by the calling to trust God to help us, not with large undertakings, but to help us through the next day, the next hour, the next minute, the next breath. Paul continually reminds us to remember that Jesus is our solution – our only solution!

> *Therefore, since we are surrounded by such a great cloud of witnesses, let us throw off everything that hinders and the sin that so easily entangles. And let us run with perseverance the race marked out for us,*
>
> —Hebrews 12:1

The Adventurous Race
It Is Not Boring. That Is For Sure!

As most of us have learned, mankind's life experiences are not always effortless. It is safe to say they are rarely so. Mankind's paths are not always straight.

God promises His children victory, but nowhere does He promise us a problem-free life. An obvious assumption about victory — defined as triumph, conquest, and winning — is that it only results from a fight. The Word of God contains many promises for those who trust Him. In my opinion, one of the most outstanding is that Christians are promised victorious lives!

The daily activities of our lives can rarely be compared to skiing down a smooth, snow-covered mountain on the slopes of the Colorado Rockies. More appropriately, life is like a roller coaster, with its ups and downs and curves of all shapes and forms. This can sure make life exciting and thrilling. The challenges can be exhilarating at times — terrifying at others.

Life can more appropriately be compared to a slip and slide on a summer day! One moment we are up and sliding forward, the next we are sliding on our backsides. Only God knows where He will take us in our lives.

With every step, we proceed through life attempting to achieve our desires to be victorious and reach the goals that we have set for ourselves. Amazingly, this often requires one thing – not that we compete, not that we run, not even that we walk – but that we stand – simply STAND.

What an incredible accomplishment just standing can be. Paul, the apostle, exhorted the Ephesians in this way:

> *Finally, be strong in the Lord and in His mighty power. Put on the full armor of God, so that you can take your stand against the devil's schemes. And, after you have done everything, to stand. Therefore, put on the full armor of God, so that when the day of evil comes, you may be able to stand your ground, and after you have done everything, to stand.*

> —Ephesians 6:10-11, 13

It is important that we take note of this ancient advice. Paul petitioned the Ephesians to stand firm in their faith in Christ to stand — just stand. He did not tell them that they needed to run, to sprint, or even to stroll. He told them to stand.

Paul's instruction is just as valid today as it was when he wrote it in his letter to the Ephesians. If you trust Christ, you can be encouraged that He will make you victorious as you progress through your race... even if you cannot do more than stand.

A Wise Pose

Have you come to the point where you understand that although Jesus is delighted to see your willingness to accomplish the goals He has given you, His ultimate desire is to see you attain them by His design, by resting in His arms and letting Him carry you to your next destination. He promises to carry you to and through your dreams and all of the routes you take on the way.

He wants to carry us to our goals and to our destinies, as well as through what appears as jungles, valleys, and mountainous terrain we may encounter along the way. He knows — more than we do — of our need for Him in the adventurous expeditions we undertake.

I can hear you now. Oh, get real! He wants to do what? He wants to carry me? If that is so, why did He give me legs? Why did he give me a will? Why did He give me a brain? If I don't make my life happen, then nobody will!

Let's meditate on the Word before we take matters into our own hands.

> *Come to me, all you who are weary and burdened, and I will give you rest.*
>
> — Matthew 11:28

Let Him Carry You!

Learn to let Him carry you. Whether you know it or not, He already does. Yes, He carries you … because you need Him to carry you. He carries you through all of life's seasons … through your small undertakings… through your adventures….and your daily agendas, even if they become monotonous. He carries you to your victories.

He wants to walk beside you daily, taking pleasure from your trust in Him and your love for others. He wants to direct your footsteps along the paths that life takes you.

At the end of Paul's life, he acknowledged that the path the Lord had him on had been a real fight, as he had been called by God to preach the Gospel to a world that did not want to hear it and hated him for it. Through it all, he still had not given up on God. One of the last things he said to his spiritual son, Timothy, was:

> *I have fought the good fight, I have finished the race, I have kept the faith. Now there is in store for me the crown of righteousness, which the Lord, the righteous Judge, will award to me on that day - and not only to me, but also to all who have longed for His appearing.*

> — II Timothy 4:7-8

Paul was a conqueror. So are you!

Scriptures

"Therefore, since we are surrounded by such a great cloud of witnesses, let us throw off everything that hinders and the sin that so easily entangles. And let us run with perseverance the race marked out for us," Hebrews 12:1

"And whatever you do, whether in word or deed, do it all in the name of the Lord Jesus, giving thanks to God the Father through him." Colossians 3:17

"But thanks be to God, who always leads us as captives in Christ's triumphal procession and uses us to spread the aroma of the knowledge of Him everywhere." 2 Corinthians 2:14

Come to me, all you who are weary and burdened, and I will give you rest." Matthew 11:28

Reflections

1. Do you see your life as a race that you will win if you just persist and trust God as you confront challenges? Why or why not?

_____

_____

_____

2. Are you able to be peaceful in your challenges because you know that God will make you victorious through each challenge if you trust Him? Why do you trust Him?

_____

_____

_____

If you don't trust Him, what is keeping you from it?

_____

_____

_____

3. If you are facing large challenges in your current situation what can you do to be more optimistic and excited about overcoming them?

_____

_____

_____

IV

THE OPPORTUNITY OF A LIFETIME
IT IS ULTIMATELY A DECISION

God's love for His children is amazing. His ability to bless us and fashion our lives is immeasurable. However, there is one action we must take daily. We're required to make a choice. Whether we acknowledge it or not, we already make it ... daily.

The choice? Will we allow Christ to reign over our hearts. It is a bit like a verse from Shakespeare: "to be or not to be." Because of God's love for us, He leaves the choice to us. When making our decisions, the options we have are limited, but challenging.

So, what is our first option? It's a choice to live our lives, not through our own understanding, but with complete trust in God for direction and fulfillment. We can trust that He will guide us... trust Him to protect us... trust Him to meet our needs. We can believe in His promise to fulfill the desires that He gives us, no matter how unbelievable they may seem. This exhibits our faith in the God that became man for us, in the form of Jesus. He is pleased with our willingness to believe that He is faithful to help us do what He told us we can do.

In choosing to trust Him, we are preparing for a spiritual heart transplant. We are being set free in Christ as our hearts are renewed. He enables us to choose daily to let go of our hurts, let go of our resentments, and let go of the inner battles we've had with ourselves. In serving Christ, we must choose to release our anger and let go of past mistakes. We have the choice to believe God's promise to bless those who serve Him with blessings that are "exceeding abundantly above all we can ever ask or think" in the midst of difficult trials (Ephesians 3:20).

What is the alternative? We can choose to fight our own battles... at least try to do so. We can hang onto resentments, past hurts and those scars we've earned so painfully. We have every right to cling tightly to our agendas and self-made plans, as well as those goals that just haven't seemed to materialize. We do all this with the hope that someday we will figure out the "why's" of life. We can hold onto our self-defense mechanisms that we've so carefully developed, in hopes that they will help us support the theories that we've created on why we should excel — because we 'deserve' to excel – because we have performed to excel.

If the latter is you, God wants you to know that He is a God who makes a way where there is no way in His children's lives. Although our plans do not always come to fruition, we can be confident that the plans God has for us are much better for us than the plans we have for ourselves.

God declared to the world, through the prophet Isaiah, that it is He who "tends his flock like a shepherd gathers the lambs in his arms and carries them close to his heart." (Isaiah 40:11). And, He "has measured the waters in the hollow of his hand" (Isaiah 40:12)

God lovingly tells us: "...do not fear, for I have redeemed you; I have summoned you by name. You are mine. When you pass through the waters, I will be with you; and when you pass through the rivers, they will not sweep over you. When you walk through the fire, you will not be burned; the flames will not set you ablaze." (Isaiah 43:1-2)

King David exemplified one who chose to trust God through times of difficult trials. In expressing his trust, he prayed "But you, LORD, are a shield around me, my glory, the One who lifts my head high." (Psalm 3:3) By the way, at the time of that prayer, David was fleeing from an oppressor who was trying to kill him—Absalom—his own son.

Interestingly, the concept of one's king being considered a

shield and protector was a common concept in ancient Israel. The psalmist rejoiced in the Lord as his royal Provider and Protector, knowing that only God could give him victory over his enemies. He believed God to be his King!

Will you walk with Him today? It's up to you. He allows you to decide if you'll make Him the King of your heart. The choice is yours. It's your prerogative.

Will you try to fight your own battles? You might be tempted to do so if you are a driven person and don't mind facing a tough challenge to succeed in what you are doing. However, at the risk of sounding negative, I can't keep from sharing what I have learned about this option. The path offers burnout, frustration and disappointment as its side orders. Believe me, it always takes a toll!

By contrast, developing a strong trust in God is a lifelong learning process. Our walks with Him include learning to abandon our worries while trusting Him. It also includes learning to sing, learning to laugh, and learning to cry. A few of the benefits are peace, joy and confidence.

Today, should you decide to serve Jesus Christ as your King, be encouraged, even joyful. The children of God are assured that they will never go hungry, never be alone, and never walk through difficult times without His support… no matter how hard circumstances seem to get. God promises that He will never leave you or forsake you. He promises that He will bless you if you choose to walk with Him.

God has wonderful plans for you. He can create a masterpiece of your life through the experiences that He allows you to have. What is His ultimate reward for those who trust in Him? Everlasting life!

Scriptures

"Come to me, all you who are weary and burdened, and I will give you rest. Take my yoke upon you and learn from me, for I am gentle and humble in heart, and you will find rest for your souls. For my yoke is easy and my burden is light." Matthew 11:28-30

"Trust in the Lord with all of your heart and lean not on your own understanding; in all your ways submit to Him, and He will make your paths straight." Proverbs 3:5-6

"For I know the plans I have for you", declares the Lord, "plans to prosper you and not to harm you, plans to give you a hope and a future." Jeremiah 29:11

Reflections

1. Think of a time when you felt like giving up while going through a trial.

   Did you choose to trust God and not give in to despair?

   How did you do it?

   _____

   _____

   _____

2. Think of a time (or many times) that you chose to trust God in a situation although everything in your mind and emotions told you not to.

   What did you experience as a result?

   _____

   _____

   _____

3. Think of a time when you were tempted to do something that you knew was not God's will.

Did you choose not to take that step against God's will because you knew that He would bless you for obeying Him?

4. If you have not trusted Jesus as your Savior and do not know how to trust God, ask yourself why you do not trust Him.

   Why is it hard to trust God?

   _____

   _____

   _____

   Do you think you'll ever be able to trust Him? Why or why not?

   _____

   _____

   _____

V

HIDDEN WITH CHRIST IN GOD

For in Him all things were created: things in heaven and on earth, visible and invisible, whether thrones or powers or rulers or authorities; all things have been created through Him and for Him.

—Colossians 1:16

What is your faith based on? Is it the depth and simplicity of Christ's truth? Or, is it based on seemingly impressive ideas of religion and what you can do to please God? Don't be deceived! Intellectualism can sound good. But, be vigilant!

Let's take a look at Paul's letter to members of a congregation who had been gradually deceived by the world's doctrine of man's justification through works. The doctrine included human regulations which included strict religious rules that no one could possibly follow.

The people were the Colossians. They met in Colossae, an ancient city in Asia Minor. In his letter, Paul advises them to avoid the pitfalls of trusting in philosophy instead of Christ.

Throughout the letter to the Colossians, Paul articulates many truths critical to understanding Christ's sufficiency. The goal of Paul's letter was to reiterate to the Colossians who Christ really is. He does that by telling them that the rewards of life can be found in Christ... only in Christ.

Our exercise, here, is to sit back and grasp the wonders of God's power and His love for His creation.

Paul reminds the Colossians to exalt Christ as the All-in-All — the Creator of the Earth — the Firstborn of all creation — the Perfect Image of God in bodily form — the pre-existing Sustainer of all good things and the Head of the Church. He said to do this in comparison to believing in the emptiness of human philosophy.

He warns the Colossians not to be deceived by heretical teachings of false humility that they were being fed by the intellectuals and religious people of the times. He tells them not to let anyone judge them by these measures because they are empty teachings, hollow of all truth and value.

Paul informs the Colossians how they can recognize the deceivers. He teaches them to watch out for some very specific characteristics in those who would lead them astray.

The heretics and intellectuals went into great detail about

what they had seen and done. They preached the law and man's regulations as the way of truth. They preached that God would reject individuals if they didn't meet the stated standards. And, finally, they stressed emphatically that intellectualism was the way to Christ. Paul called the minds of these people "puffed up" with idle notions.

These worldly theories are still taught today. That is why the Book of Colossians is so encouraging to Christ-seekers. We are free in Christ!

The beautiful truths that Paul teaches us include that all things, in heaven and on the earth, were created by Christ and for Christ. He tells us that Christ has supremacy over all things. The term "all things" includes the good and the bad plus the visible and invisible — whether "thrones or powers or rulers or authorities." Everything was created by Christ and for Christ

Paul tells us that all things are held together by Jesus. Hidden in Christ are all treasures of wisdom and knowledge. Wow! It requires some intense thought to soak these truths into our minds and hearts.

Colossians – Personalized

I like Paul's style of writing. He seems to know we can be a bit slow at times. He reiterates to the Colossians that Christ is the fullness of the deity in bodily form. He reminds them that Christ replaced all human regulations as the path to justification. And, he reminds them that Christ is the only way to receive God's approval and forgiveness of sins.

> *For God was pleased to have all His fullness dwell in Him, and through Him, to reconcile to Himself all things, whether things on earlier or things in heaven, by making peace through His blood, shed on the cross.*

> — Colossians 1:19-20

Paul continues to teach the Colossians that none of man's philosophies, promoting any knowledge or ideas outside of Christ, are worth anything. He does not want anyone to deceive themselves with fine-sounding arguments. He continually communicates the same message: "when we were dead in sin, God made us alive in Christ." (Colossians 2:13)

Christ's Triumphal Celebration

Paul, in Colossians, informs us that Jesus disarmed all evil powers — triumphing over them at the cross. The picture Paul paints here is that Jesus took Satan and his demons, stripped them of their clothes and weapons, and made a public spectacle of them. "And having disarmed the powers and authorities, he made a public spectacle of them, triumphing over them by the cross." (Colossians 2:15) This triumphal process caused them to look like a group of defeated soldiers, paraded around for all to see. Now, doesn't that just make you want to laugh? It does me.

Christ's Victory is Our Victory!

As recipients of the victory Christ won on the cross for Mankind, we are told that we are risen with Christ from the dead. Paul tells us to keep our hearts and minds set on things above, where Christ is seated at the right hand of God, and not on the things of the Earth. Paul tells us we can do this because we are dead to this world and alive in Christ. We are "hidden with Christ in God." Paul also says Christ came to earth, was crucified, and rose from the dead, so that when He appears at the second coming, we can appear with Him in Glory.

Our Final Calling

Why would any of us allow the world to pressure us into believing we must meet their standards for acceptance? Only for selfish reasons! Watch out!

Remember this. If Jesus Christ is your Lord, you serve the All-in-All. You serve the One who has supremacy over all things. Those who love Jesus serve the One who all things are created for, created by, and created through.

You are hidden with Christ in God!

Scriptures

"Since, then, you have been raised with Christ, set your heart on things above, where Christ is, seated at the right hand of God. For you died, and your life is now hidden with Christ in God." Colossians 3:1, 3

"Let the peace of Christ rule in your hearts, since as members of one body you were called to peace. And, be thankful." Colossians 3:15

Reflections

1. Do you feel that you have to do something to earn God's love and His approval?
   Do you try to please Him with your actions? If you said yes, how did you do that?

2. Do you understand that Jesus loves you so much that He has disarmed all evil powers, triumphing over them at the cross, so that you can have eternal salvation and peace while you are on Earth?
   If you have a hard time grasping that, why?

3. Do you feel that God loves you so much that He protects you from the attacks of Satan and his demons to ruin your life?
   If not, what would it take for Him to prove that to you?

VI

JUST BE HELD

There remains a Sabbath rest for the people of God; for anyone who enters God's rest also rests from their works, just as God did from His.

— Hebrews 4:9-10

God's love for mankind is so deep that we will never be able to grasp the depth of it until Jesus returns or takes us home. Understanding that truth is a lifetime aspiration for many people as we get closer to the day that He will personally tell us "Well done, my good and faithful servant!" (Matthew 25:21)

Have you ever had a hard time letting yourself rest in the peace that the Lord gives His children? Is it tough for you to believe that your circumstances will work out well if you don't control the situation? Do you find it hard to believe that you can meet your goals without striving to make them happen?

Speaking openly, I am embarrassed to say that although I've grasped the truth of His love and learned to rest in Him through my challenges, my rest has usually been temporary.

Through introspection, I've realized that I've made many of my decisions because I haven't understood the level of God's love for me and His willingness to take care of me through my situations without my help. Wow… that was tough to admit.

I know that the only thing which enables me to remain strong is the ability that the Lord gives me to stand firm through life's storms. However, the strength He has given me to stand has also enabled me to feel that I can use my control to hold things together and reach my goals without His help, many times. The constant messages I tell myself include "I have to be strong… I have to hang on … I have to press forward to reach my goals…. I must meet the expectations of family, bosses, friends or… (fill in the blank). These ideas have made themselves comfortable in my head too many times.

Along with allowing me many wonderful experiences, Jesus has led me through many tough terrains while I've faced the challenges of life. God's paths for me have always resulted in victories, although I might not have seen them as victories when I was going through them.

After many years of living the Christian life, I've realized that God is still opening my spiritual eyes. Recently, the Lord has used a contemporary Christian song called "Just Be Held" to remind me of how deep His love is for me. It is a song in which the artist portrays God as a Father saying, "My child, stop fighting. Trust me. I will not let you fall."

A few years ago, while I was recovering from surgery for breast cancer, I faced the challenge of determining whether to have another medical procedure. It was a hard decision. One day, I heard "Just Be Held". Although I had heard the song many times, I had not personalized it.

On this day, the Lord made that song very personal to me. He showed me that I could stop stressing because He was going to help me make the right decision. He was taking care of me and He would make whatever I decided work out good for me.

After that day, although I still did not know what surgery to choose, I decided to trust God to give me the wisdom to make the right decision when it was time.

You're Not Always in Control

Stop thinking that you need to control your situation. Stop thinking that you need to use your strengths and talents to create success in your current circumstances.

I don't know about you, but it has taken me years to believe that God simply wants to be with me... to spend time with me ... to carry my burdens... so much that He wants to just hold me like a father does his baby. But He really does!

I've have believed this truth for others and I have loved encouraging them that God loves them. I've helped individuals celebrate that the Lord wants them to always have His joy and peace, no matter what they may go through. I confidently tell all who will listen that their solution is merely to trust God and take joy in knowing how much He loves them. But, I must admit that it has been a real challenge for me to do so.

Let's get down to the facts. It's not about what we can do to get the best results, or what we can do to try to make things work things out for us, or even what we need to do to please the Lord. It is about what He can do for us and about how much He yearns to do those things.

God's willingness and desire to hold His children and take care of us is one aspect of His grace. His invitation to hold us securely in His arms is an expression of His love to the fullest!

We need to rest in our efforts and trust that God is in control of our lives. We must surrender the idea that only our efforts will bring the results we want... and need. We need to let Him hold us.

Let's accept this truth today. Let's rest in His love. What an amazing concept!

Now, go on and spend some time with your Father. He is waiting for you!

Scriptures

"The LORD your God is with you, the Mighty Warrior who saves. He will take great delight in you; in His love He will no longer rebuke you but will rejoice over you with singing." Zephaniah 3:17

"Whoever dwells in the shelter of the Most High will rest in the shadow of the Almighty. I will say of the LORD, "He is my refuge and my fortress; my God, in whom I will trust." Psalm 91:1-2

"Commit your way to the Lord; trust in Him and He will do this: He will make your righteous reward shine like the dawn, your vindication like the noonday sun. Rest in the Lord and wait patiently for Him." Psalm 37:5-6

"Wait for the LORD; be strong and take heart and wait for the LORD." Psalm 27:14

Reflections

1. Do you know what it means to "rest in God"? If so, what does it feel like to rest in Him?

    _____

    _____

    _____

2. Do you think that you are in control of everything in your life? If you find that you always have to be in control, what do you think would happen if you let go?

    _____

    _____

    _____

3. Think of a time when you trusted God enough to believe that He was on your side and He would take care of you without your help. What gave you that confidence in Him?

If you have never had that confidence in God, what has kept you from it?

_____

_____

_____

VII

MIRACULOUS RESTORATION

Valley of Dry Bones
(Ezekiel 37)

Prayer. Trusting God for the concerns of our lives. Opening our hearts before Him. Believing that God knows and cares about His children's concerns — large and small. Believing that God has the power and will to act on behalf of His children, to restore them, and to revive them! These are man's callings.

I don't know about you, but I require His gentle lessons quite frequently. Several years ago, the Lord reminded me, in an interesting manner, that His restorative nature was as true in my life in the 21st century as it was for the Israelites of the Old Testament.

I call the manner He used "interesting" because, although I had spent many years studying the Bible, one

Sunday morning in 2002, He had me reading the Bible in a personally unchartered territory— the Old Testament book of Ezekiel.

In 2001 and 2002, I went through some serious emotional challenges when I experienced a broken relationship, a career move due to an economic downturn, and a move into a new home.

That Sunday morning, I was encouraged by a unique experience in which the Lord showed me, once again, that He would make me victorious and bless me in the areas I knew the devil intended to steal from me.

God reinforced that He would make my life better than it was before. I just needed to trust Him. I needed to remember that our God has supernatural power...with no limits.

Although I had been saved for more than fifteen years, I had rarely referenced the book of Ezekiel. Yet, that morning, I was confronted with this unique message of God's love and power towards His children three times. I was blessed to be reminded that I served an Almighty God who specialized in doing extraordinary acts in the restoration of His kids.

He has put it on my heart to share my "Ezekiel 37" experience with others who might need a little reminder of God's love for them and His power to act on their behalf. I hope you are encouraged!

Three Amazing Reminders –
One Quiet Sunday Morning

One Sunday morning in 2002, I woke up early. I immediately felt impressed to read Ezekiel 37. In this chapter, God tells the prophet Ezekiel to speak life into a valley of very dry bones. Due to Ezekiel's obedience, God brought the bones of these people back to life.

In the passage, God tells Ezekiel,

> *Prophesy to these bones and say to them, 'Dry bones, hear the word of the LORD! This is what the Sovereign LORD says to these bones: I will make breath enter you, and you will come to life. I will attach tendons to you and make flesh come upon you and cover you with skin; I will put breath in you, and you will come to life. Then you will know that I am the LORD.'*

— Ezekiel 37:4-9

What Ezekiel saw next would shock anyone. The Bible says that, as he was prophesying, there was a rattling sound. The bones were coming together, bone to bone. When he looked at them, he saw their tendons and flesh appear. He also saw that skin covered them, but they still weren't breathing.

God told Ezekiel to breathe into the slain, that they may live. When Ezekiel spoke the words, "breath entered them" and they came to life."

We Shall Live

The Lord had a message that He wanted Israel to understand. He told them "I will put my Spirit in you and you will live, and I will settle you in your own land. Then you will know that I, the LORD, have spoken, and I have done it." He later tells them: "My tabernacle shall be with them, and I will be their God and they shall be my people". Ezekiel 37:13-14, 27

The passage goes on to explain that dry bones represent the house of Israel. God loved His children so much that He was willing to look past their sins to deliver them out of the graves they had dug for themselves.

Today, we can rejoice in the mercy He showed Israel. He is the same God for us! Our Heavenly Father is willing to deliver us out of the messes we create for ourselves. Now, that is mercy!

When I realized that it was through Ezekiel's obedience that the bones came to life, I realized that obedience was my solution, too. I needed to have the obedience to look the impossible in the face, stand up to discouragement and put my hope in the Lord.

A Preacher on the Radio

Within the hour, I tuned the radio to a Christian station and couldn't believe what I was hearing. The pastor was speaking on Ezekiel 37 and God's restorative nature. Encouraged and almost in tears, I thought, "Wow! God must really want me to get this message!"

Later, I was amazed, yet again, when I went to church. The pastor was speaking on none other than Ezekiel 37 and how God revived the valley of dry bones. The pastor's message reiterated how God has the same power and desire to restore the lives of His children today as He did when reviving Israel.

I was reduced to tears. I was in awe at the encouragement I received from God that morning, from a very unexpected source.

Even when we think we've failed, God has plans for us that are far greater than we can imagine. Whenever life takes us down paths that make no sense to us, we must still trust God. I found God's love and merciful actions toward Israel to be a great example.

God's Mercy and Love

The book of Ezekiel has taken on a new meaning for me. It had never been a book that I often considered studying.

That morning, I learned it is full of God's truths that can be applied to life today.

In one single morning, I was reminded to trust God for the large and small cares of my life. In a marvelous way, He was lovingly reminding me that He was able and willing to bless me by bringing His will to pass in my life. I realized that His will contains the best life for me. I celebrated His power to lead His children ever forward.

What? Dallas Theological Seminary?

Soon after my "Ezekiel 37" awakening, God had another surprise around the corner. He wasn't done revealing His love to me through Ezekiel.

A few months after that morning, I found myself in a place in which I had never considered going. A friend of mine was thinking of attending Dallas Theological Seminary. She asked if I would ride to Dallas with her to visit for a day. We lived in Austin. I accepted her invitation.

We spent the day learning about the programs, meeting professors and attending classes. In the afternoon, we wanted to attend a specific class. When we walked into the room it was full of students. There were no empty spaces. So, we decided to go with Plan B and sit in the class next door where the topic was the Old Testament. When we stepped into the room, the students were actively listening to a song and reading the lyrics projected on the chalkboard.

Much to my amazement, the title of the song was "Ezekiel 37". Is God amazing or what?

I was in awe that God loved me so much that He would take me almost 200 miles to show me that His restoration power was always mine. He had lovingly led my steps to that room on that day… 3 hours away from my home … to show me that my life was in His hands and He had a great plan for me.

Your Restoration

His restoration power and His ability to deliver you is yours, right now! Jesus holds your life and your dreams in His hands. We should be bold in our prayers and thank Him for bringing His will to pass in our lives. That includes our petitions to Him to help us believe His plans for us are better than our own

If God chose to restore the house of Israel, despite their sins, what will He do for His children today? He will restore us and bless us in ways beyond our imaginations!

Scriptures

"Whoever has the Son has life; whoever does not have the Son of God does not have life." 1 John 5:12

"He who was seated on the throne said, "I am making everything new!" Revelations 21:5

"Jesus looked at them and said, 'With man this is impossible, but with God all things are possible.'" Matthew 19:26

Reflections

1. Have you ever been so disappointed in something that you felt you could never have hope that the Lord would give you success in that area again?
   If you have experienced this, how did you regain your hope in God?

   _____

   _____

   _____

If you have not regained hope, explain what is keeping you from believing God for it.

_____

_____

_____

2. Have you ever had so much hope in something other than God that you would feel lost if you did not have it?

_____

_____

_____

If that "something" is, or was, not God, what made you have so much hope in that "something"?

_____

_____

_____

What would make you trust God again?

_____

_____

_____

3. Do you believe that the Lord can restore you from the losses you've had in life?
   If not, what would it take for God to convince you that He can restore you?

_____

_____

_____

VIII

HE STILL ROLLS THE STONE

Who will roll the stone away from the entrance
of the tomb? But when they looked up, they saw
that the stone, which was very large, had been
rolled away.

—Mark 16:3-4

Have you ever been ready to give up on what you consider to
be your God-inspired dreams? Have you felt led to take on a
project that seemed impossible? Maybe you've faced serious
discouragement because life isn't what you have wanted it to
be. If so, take heart in the power of the Lord Jesus!

The stone that was placed in front of Jesus' tomb with
the purpose of sealing Him inside could not keep the Lord
from fulfilling His plans. His power was so great that not
even physical death could keep Jesus from serving the will
of His Father.

Why Do We Doubt That God Can Fulfill Our Wildest Dreams?

Are you afraid of failure? Are you afraid that others might think you're a bit crazy for having goals beyond what they believe you should have? Has anyone ever suggested that you are audacious for even thinking you could achieve the goals you have?

It was no problem for Jesus to miraculously feed 4,000 men and their families, with seven loaves and a few little fish, on a day that they had come together to listen to Him. (Matthew 15:32-38) At another time, He fed 5,000 men and their families with five loaves of bread and two fish. (Matthew 14:16-21) If that doesn't prove that God makes His power available to those who trust in Him I don't know what does. Why would we doubt that He wants to fulfill our deepest dreams?

Do Not Give Up on God — He Doesn't Give Up on You

God wants His children to trust Him because His will for our lives is the best outcome we can ask for. Keep praying and trusting the Lord for your future. Trust Him with your cares and concerns. Tell Him about your dreams and your desires.

No challenge is too great for Him! Life is many times beyond our understanding. Don't let Satan intimidate you and stop you from pursuing the dreams you feel that God has given you – even when they seem like they are more of a challenge than you feel you can take on. Be assured, when God calls, He qualifies. His power enables you to press on!

> *For God's gifts and His call are irrevocable.*

> —Romans 11:29

His Love for You is Amazing!

In sending out the twelve disciples, Jesus told them not to fear. He shared with them how much their Father loved them. He told them that the level of the Father's love for them was so great that the very hairs on their heads were numbered.

> *Are not two sparrows sold for a penny? Yet, not one of them will fall to the ground outside of your Father's care. And, even the very hairs of your head are all numbered.*

> —Matthew 10:29-30

God's love for us is amazing! How can we ever doubt His

care for us? Why do we question His faithfulness to bring His plans to pass in our lives? As we walk in obedience to Him, we can trust that God will direct us and lead us into His purpose 'not by might nor by power, but by His spirit.' (Zechariah 4:6)

Surrender Your Heart

Your Father is the Giver of life and breath. Scripture teaches us that He governs the universe and all of creation, including all creatures – both men and animals. Throughout the Bible, Jesus is called the Ruler of all things, the Blessed One, the Redeemer and the One and Only God.

He knows the plans He has for you and that His purposes will prevail. We, as part of His creation, must let go and surrender to His will. The Bible offers plenty of excellent examples of how God has made His people victorious through difficult times. A few well-known biblical overcomers are Joseph, King David, Job, Abraham, Moses, St. Paul and the ultimate overcomer, Jesus Christ.

In their hearts, humans plan their course, but the Lord establishes their steps.

—Proverbs 16:9

God Desires for You to Rest in His Peace – Even in the Stormy Waves of Life

King David referred to God's peace as "green pastures" and "still waters" in Psalm 23:2. Doesn't that sound restful? The bible assures us that, regardless of the adversities we face, we can walk in joy and an abundance of peace in Christ.

> *And, we know that in all things God works for the good of those who love him, who have been called according to His purpose.*

> —Romans 8:28

Moreover, God can do the impossible for you. No challenge is too great for God to fulfill. No event is too large for Him to orchestrate.

You can rest in Christ today. Put your faith in Him. In challenging times, remember how Jesus transformed dinner for a few into a feast for thousands. Jesus rose from the dead. He can handle our challenges, too!

> *Now to Him who is able to do exceedingly abundantly above all that we ask or think, according to the power that works in us to Him*

*be glory in the church by Christ Jesus to all
generations, forever and ever. Amen.*

—Ephesians 3:20

Scriptures

"There was a violent earthquake, for an angel of the Lord came down from heaven and, going to the tomb, rolled back the stone and sat on it." Matthew 28:2

"When He had said this, Jesus called in a loud voice, "Lazarus, come out!" The dead man came out, his hands and feet wrapped with strips of linen, and a cloth around his face. Jesus said to them, "Take off the grave clothes and let him go." John 11:43-44

"He took her by the hand and said to her, *"Talitha koum!"* (which means "Little girl, I say to you, get up!"). Immediately, the girl stood up and began to walk around (she was twelve years old). At this they were completely astonished." Mark 5:41-42

Reflections

1. The people who were mentioned in John 11:43 and Mark 5:42 had one thing in common: They had died,

but miraculously became alive when they were touched
by Jesus.

Do you believe that God can do the same today? Why
do you believe that He can or that He cannot?

_____

_____

_____

2. Have you ever had a life dream on which you have given
   up because it has not come to fruition?

   If you have, what made you give up on that dream?

_____

_____

_____

What must happen for you to dream again?

_____

_____

_____

3. Do you believe that Jesus can and wants to do miracles in your life?

   If you don't believe that, what would it take for you to believe it?

   _____

   _____

   _____

IX

THE VEIL REMOVED

Whenever anyone turns to the Lord, the veil is taken away.

—2 Corinthians 3:16

Do you see God as a distant ruler? Or do you see God as a father who is so close to his children that he will never leave them ... no matter what they do? If you believe that the Bible is true you can believe that God loves you more than the perfect father.

Can you see that today is a blessing — a gift that cannot be replaced? Or, do you see it as just another humdrum period of twenty-four hours? We usually base the value of our days on the experiences we encounter on those days... pleasant or unpleasant, easy or hard, fun or painful.

This moment is invaluable! No matter whether you see

today as a blessing or a curse, the truth is that each day is remarkable. It will never reoccur!

I encourage you to take advantage of every opportunity you have right now. No matter what we have experienced, or what we are in the midst of experiencing, we are blessed with the life that only God can give us. No matter what you are going through today, it is wise to live with the mindset that today will be a positive experience.

Today vs Tomorrow

Have you ever found yourself believing that your joy lies in experiences in the future? Have you felt your dreams might be impossible since they haven't manifested yet and you don't know if the Lord will choose to fulfill them?

Do you believe that the only way you can reach your goals is if you make them happen, yet you don't have the capability to bring them to fruition?

You're not alone. These thoughts have taken up residence in my mind... many times. However, I've learned that God will give me peace if I believe He is faithful to His promises and He promises to make His children victorious. As the Bible says, His promises are Yes and Amen.

As Christians, we can believe that our lives are full of exciting future opportunities. More importantly, we can bathe in the blessings that the Lord has bestowed on us each moment today.

Today vs. Yesterday

Regret should not be a regular part of our lives. We should not compare what we have today with what had yesterday. The events of yesterday do not determine what will happen today.

Our abilities and limitations of yesterday have no bearing on today. We should never let regret rob us of our hope for today or tomorrow.

As we walk in gratefulness for the blessings of yesterday, we must remember that time doesn't stand still. A new day is coming!

Forget What Lies Behind
Don't Worry About Tomorrow

In order to enjoy today, we must refuse to live in the past and not allow ourselves to fear the future.

Planning is a good thing. I can confidently say that life without planning is chaos. But I have learned that we must not be so convinced that our plans are the best way to get where we want to go that we are distraught if our lives take us down different roads.

We must realize how blessed we are right now... this very minute! We must have hope for our future, and we can be excited for our future if we choose to be excited about today.

If we trust the Lord, we can be confident that God has our lives in His hands. He is the one who walked us through our yesterdays. He is the one with our future in His hands. And, He will be with us as we experience this wonderful thing called Today.

> *Take delight in the Lord, and He will give you the desires of your heart.*
>
> —Psalm 37:4

Scriptures

"But whenever anyone turns to the Lord, the veil is taken away." 2 Corinthians 3:16

"Many are the plans in a person's heart, but it is the LORD's purpose that prevails." Proverbs 19:21

"The LORD delights in those who fear him, who put their hope in His unfailing love." Psalm 147:11

"When I saw Him, I fell at his feet as though dead. Then He placed His right hand on me and said: Do not be afraid. I am the First and the Last. I am the Living One; I was dead, and now look, I am alive for ever and ever! And I hold the keys of death and Hades." Revelations 1:17-18

Reflections

1. How much time do you spend worrying about your future or regretting things done in the past? Is there one area of concern that you worry about the most? Why?

_____

_____

_____

Will you let yourself receive God's forgiveness?

_____

_____

_____

Will you forgive others who have hurt you?

_____

_____

_____

2. Do you find that you are frequently concerned, or overconcerned, about your future? If so, what areas do you find yourself concerned about the most? Why?

_____

_____

_____

3. What would it take for you to trust that God is in control of your life and He can help you conquer your challenges?

_____

_____

_____

X

REST IN HIM

As a citizen of the 21st century, I have had an ongoing issue which I think you might have experienced. I am referring to my tendency to refuse to let myself rest and trust the Lord to take care of my concerns. I have realized that I must stop pressuring myself to control my situations if I am to live the life that I want... the life of peace that God has promised to give me. It is important to know we have been commanded by God to lay down our burdens and rest in Him.

Allow me to ask – have you have experienced periods of stress, anxiety or doubt. I have, and I don't know of anyone who hasn't. My version of this includes a strong feeling that I always need to do more to get where I want to go in life.

There have been many times when I've held onto self-imposed pressures that I must do more to make something happen before I can rest. These feelings have been related to my home life, my work life, something for the family, something for friends, something for ministry, something for the community, etc. I also want to spend time in prayer and Bible study to strengthen my relationship with the Lord.

Do this thing. Finish that thing. Go work out. Call that person. Call another person. Read this email... and another email... and another email. Eat this. Don't eat that. It is never-ending.

What are the consequences of all these options? Could there be a simpler way? You bet!

Stop! Relax! Rest!

I've learned that the only way to find my resting place is to believe that the Lord is in control of my life, even when I don't understand how. My peace comes from trusting that Jesus has a wonderful plan for my life. He will use all of my former and current experiences to make me better as He brings my future to pass.

You, too, can rest and be confident that Jesus loves you as you are. As a Christian, you can rest in knowing that He is working on your behalf. You can relax in knowing that, although you might not be where you want to be, Jesus is working behind the scenes to make His perfect will come to pass. His plan for you is always better than your own.

When we trust the Lord, we can rest assured that

everything is going to be alright. As we are promised in Romans 8:28, God will work all things out for the good of them that love Him.

One of the most important reminders of our calling is to rest in God's grace. The writer of the book of Hebrews says that God's rest is available to us. He also emphasizes that we cannot please God if we don't take advantage of His rest. We do not please the Lord if we don't rest in Him.

The Israelites did not enter the Promised Land because they let the concerns of their world keep them from trusting the Lord. The Lord did one miracle after another to show them how much He loved them. He split the sea for the Israelites to walk through. He sent them bread and meat from the sky. He gave them water from a rock. They had every reason to trust Him, but they refused to trust Him.

The author Hebrews wrote that we, as Christians, must be careful that none of us fail to rest in Him. How do we rest in the Lord when everything in our world says we should stress out? Faith... walking by faith! That is how we rest!

Faith: The Main Ingredient

How can you walk in faith? First, you must know what faith is. Again, the author of Hebrews comes to the rescue. In Hebrews 11:1, he gives us a clear definition of faith: "Now faith is the substance of things hoped for, the evidence of things not seen."

When we have not yet seen our dreams come to pass with our physical eyes, we need not doubt. God will bring His perfect will to pass as we walk with Him. His will is always for the good of His children.

Contentment is Ours

When we give God control of our lives our outcomes will always be good, even if we can't see how. If you are a Christian and you live a life aimed at pleasing the Lord He says to you, "You are pleasing me as the person that I have made you to be."

The Bible clearly tells us that Jesus wants to be with us just because we are His. Don't let the things of this world and the opinions of others overtake you. Don't compare yourself to anyone! You are blessed to be able to rest in God's peace... just to rest. What a concept! Remember that!

Scriptures

"Come to me, all you who are weary and burdened, and I will give you rest." Matthew 11:28

"Be still, and know that I am God; I will be exalted among the nations, I will be exalted in the earth." Psalm 46:10

"The Lord is my shepherd, I lack nothing. He makes me lie down in green pastures. He leads me beside quiet waters. He refreshes my soul. He guides me along the right paths for His name's sakes." Psalm 23:1-3

Reflections

1. Are you able to trust that God will take care of your concerns even if you don't stress to resolve them? If not, what would it take for you to rest in Him?

_____

_____

_____

2. According to the Bible, mankind can find more peace by trusting the Lord than in anything we do on our own. Do you believe that is true? Why or why not?

_____

_____

_____

XI

DOES THE LIGHTNING REPORT TO YOU?

For centuries, mankind has exerted energy and emotions to create beauty in art. They use their creativity to produce something beautiful in the eyes of their audiences – and in their own eyes. It is almost impossible for artists to explain the level of fulfillment they receive by sharing their work with others who enjoy it and those who realize the talent used to create it.

Jesus — The Principal Artist

After I had spent months working with a group of very difficult and belittling people, I found myself extremely discouraged and tired with life. As a project manager in the technology department of a large company, I had loved my work. But, due to complications in the project and differing opinions among leadership, it had become very confrontational.

Corporate politics had resulted in the loss of my job. I was in a place where I was trying to reason things out. It had only left me with the questions "God, why did you let me go through that? What do you want me to do now?" I lacked the ability to hope that anything I could do would give me the emotional strength that I wanted.

As a Christian who has seen God's faithfulness many times, I strongly believe that the Bible is the Word of God. I believe that it is full of truths about God's power and His love for His children, both of which He uses to bring victory into our lives and overturn the devil's schemes to defeat us.

The Joy of God's Word

Soon after I lost my job, I opened my Bible to the latter part of the book of Job. The Bible says that Job had lived such a godly life that God spoke highly of him to the devil, saying he was blameless and an upright man who feared God and shunned evil. The Bible says he was the greatest man among the people of the East.

Satan challenged God. He said that Job would curse God if he went through enough pain. To prove that untrue, God said that He would allow Satan to touch every part of Job's life, but He would not allow him to kill Job. Through Satanic attacks, Job lost almost everything he had—including all of his children, all his livestock and much of his health. But he still did not curse God.

He did have a wife. She was not much help. The only consolation she provided was to tell him to curse God and die. (Don't we all need an encourager like that?) Through a supernatural faith, Job would not let those losses make him curse God and give up.

But, like us, Job was not perfect. After enduring much pain and distress, he cursed the day he was born; although he would not curse God, he started to doubt Him.

The Lord Sets Job Straight

The day I read that passage, I was contemplating what the Lord had done in my life through this terrible "job" experience. I was reminded of some passages in Job, in chapters 38 through 41, which I had loved for years. This passage is one in which the Lord responds to Job's doubt.

The Bible says that the Lord answered Job out of a whirlwind. "Who is this that obscures my plans with words without knowledge? Brace yourself like a man. I will question you, and you will answer me."

Through a series of rhetorical questions which no sane

man would have the knowledge to answer, God points out Job's prideful responses to the events that have transpired in his life. The result was Job's awe and recognition of the power and creativity of God, the Author of Life.

I had to laugh when I read those passages where God spoke to Job with what I considered a hint of sarcasm. I could almost hear Him speaking to me in the same manner… rebuking me in love… because I didn't trust Him through my pain.

During God's conversation with Job, He used humor and truth to set Job straight. He made some blunt statements about Job's audacious ideas that God owed him answers. He even called Job a man without knowledge. He was essentially saying, "child, when are you going to trust Me?" God brought Job back to reality by reminding him of how majestic and powerful He was.

> In Job 38, the Lord spoke to Job out of a storm, saying *"Where were you when I laid the earth's foundation? Who marked off its dimensions? Who stretched a measuring line across it? On what were its footings set, or who laid its cornerstone—while the morning stars sang together, and all the angels shouted for joy? Who shut up the sea behind doors when it burst forth from the womb, when I made the clouds its garment and wrapped it in thick darkness,*

when I fixed limits for it and set its doors and
bars in place?"

"Have you ever given orders to the morning, or
shown the dawn its place that it might take the
earth by the edges and shake the wicked out of it?"

"Have you journeyed to the springs of the sea
or walked in the recesses of the deep? Have the
gates of death been shown to you? Have you
comprehended the vast expanses of the earth?
Tell me, if you know all this."

"What is the way to the abode of light? And
where does darkness reside? Can you take them
to their places? Do you know the paths to their
dwellings? Do you send the lightning bolts on
their way? Who has the wisdom to count the
clouds? Surely you know, for you were already
born! You have lived so many years!"

The Lord continues to ask Job mind-boggling questions
which he could answer with nothing but "I know that You
can do all things; no purpose of yours can be thwarted.
You asked, 'Who is this that obscures my plans without
knowledge? Surely, I spoke of things that I did not understand,
things too wonderful for me to know." (Job 42:2-3).

The result of that questioning was Job's recognition that God was more powerful than he had ever imagined. He repented.

In the end, the Lord restored Job's fortunes and gave him twice as much as he had before. The Lord blessed the latter part of Job's life more than his earlier years. He gave him thousands of sheep, thousands of camels, thousands of oxen, and thousands of donkeys. He also gave him seven sons and three daughters.

The bible says that Job died an old man and full of years. He saw his children and their children to the fourth generation.

God is in Control

The Lord loves us as much as He loved Job. He is just as powerful now as He was then. We, as His children, can rest assured that He knows our situations and has the power to keep the devil from defeating us.

As God's children, we can be confident that He not only cares for us through our situations, but He will restore us with lives better than we had before our trials.

The next time you're tempted to question God's level of control in your life, or you stress out about a specific situation, remember He is working behind the scenes to mold you into a beautiful piece of art.

If you find yourself frustrated with God because He doesn't move fast enough, and He doesn't give you everything you want when you want it, be patient. He will be right with you. He is ordering the constellations and setting the moon into place!

Scriptures

"The LORD makes firm the steps of the one who delights in Him; though he may stumble, he will not fall; for the LORD upholds him with His hand." Psalm 37:23-24

"As for God, his way is perfect: The LORD's word is flawless; he shields all who take refuge in Him." Psalm 18:30

Reflections

1. Do you believe that God is working behind the scenes to bless you even though He allows you to go through hardships?
   If not, why don't you believe it?

_____

_____

_____

2. Do you believe that God has the power to restore you and the will to restore you if you trust Him with your life? How do you show your faith?

_____

_____

_____

3. What would it take for you to believe that the same God who created the universe and everything in it, including life and the galaxies, knows and loves you?

_____

_____

_____

XII

The Prize

An amazing reward awaits you! Keep your eyes on the prize!

The Bible clearly conveys that God rewards everyone who pleases Him. We are told in Hebrews 6:11 that God is a rewarder of those who diligently seek Him. According to Ephesians 3:20, we serve a God who is able to do exceedingly, abundantly above all we can ever ask or think. That amazes me!

When Jesus was preparing His disciples for the days that He would not be with them on Earth, He told them not to be discouraged. He told them He would not leave them alone. He said that He was going to prepare a home for them in Heaven... a beautiful home. Moreover, He promised them that He would come back and take them to be with Him.

> My Father's house has many rooms; if that
> were not so, I would have told you that. I am

going there to prepare a place for you. And if I go and prepare a place for you, I will come back and take you to be with me that you also may be where I am.

—John 14:2-3

God Rewards Our Faithfulness

Several years later, Jesus appeared to John, who had been exiled to the Island of Patmos because of his faith. John was the only living disciple. Jesus told Him, "Do not be afraid. I am the First and the Last. I am the Living One. I was dead, and now look, I am alive forever and ever! And I hold the keys of death and Hades." (Revelation 1:8)

In the first chapter of Revelation, John says that when he was in the Spirit he heard a loud voice like a trumpet, which said: "Write on a scroll what you see and send it to the seven churches: to Ephesus, Smyrna, Pergamum, Thyatira, Sardis, Philadelphia and Laodicea."

In those letters, Jesus gave a personal word to each of the churches. He told each group that He knew their deeds – good and bad. He expressed approval to some for their obedience and persistence, and rebuke to others who had wandered away from Him.

Throughout chapters two and three of Revelations, Jesus

lovingly ends each of the letters with a promise – a great promise! He tells them that there are heavenly rewards for those who remain faithful to Him through their trials.

The rewards He promised to those who turned to Him, returned to Him, or kept serving Him are so magnificent they are beyond our imagination. Although He made these promises to a specific group of people, the Bible says that we serve a God of impartiality. Today, these promises apply to any person who calls on Jesus to be their Lord and Savior and who does not turn away from Him.

A few of Christ's promises to the one who conquers by choosing to live for Him are listed below. They are amazing rewards!

- "I will give him the right to eat of the tree of life, which is in the paradise of God." (Revelation 2:7)
- "I will give you life as your victor's crown." (Revelation 2:10)
- "I will give them the right to sit with me on my throne, just as I was victorious and sat down with my Father on His throne." (Revelation 3:21)
- "I will never blot out the name of that person from the Book of Life but will acknowledge that name before my Father and his angels." (Revelation 3:5)
- "I will make a pillar in the temple of my God. Never again will they leave it. I will write on them the name

of my God and the name of the city of my God, the new Jerusalem, which is coming down out of heaven from my God; and I will also write on them my new name." (Revelation 3:12)

- "I will give some of the hidden manna. I will also give that person a white stone with a new name written on it, known only to the one who receives it." (Revelation 2:17)
- "I will give authority over the nations — that one will rule them with an iron scepter and will dash them to pieces like pottery — just as I have received authority from my Father. I will also give that one the morning star." (Revelation 2:26)
- "I stand at the door and knock. If anyone hears My voice and opens the door, I will come in and eat with that person, and they with Me." (Revelation 3:20)

You can be assured that great rewards await you if you serve the Lord and remain faithful to Him throughout your life.

Although all of the rewards He gives His children are wonderful, beyond our understanding, the greatest of them is His promise to tell us "Well done, my good and faithful servant."

XIII

A Final Word

Determination... Resolution... Optimism... Mercy... a "Don't Quit" attitude...These are just some of the character traits that Jesus creates in those who trust in Him.

Life consists of many choices – many roads to travel. Our lives are comprised of constant choices. We must choose which roads to take. Don't forget the ultimate choice we face daily — "How will I respond to my challenges?"

Our trust in Jesus Christ and our decisions to make Him the Lord of our lives will determine the ease at which we handle our life events. We can insist on trying to get what we want through our own power; or we can trust God through our challenges and believe that He is faithful to fulfill His promises.

We have no cause to fear if we believe Jesus to be the Savior of the world and make Him our Lord. As the children of God, we can be confident that we will make it through every battle we face with success. God is faithful to His promises.

God has promised that He will be with you and make you an overcomer as you trust Him. The Bible says that He will be your "all in all". He is your Father. He is your coach. He is your caretaker. He is your friend.

We don't understand how He can be all of those things, but we are not called to understand everything. We are called to put our total trust in Him. He promises that He will make us more than conquerors as we live out our stories.

God created you for a purpose. He is constantly using your challenges to make you an overcomer... a winner! The Lord is creating a beautiful tapestry in you.

You are a masterpiece...a conqueror of your current challenges and those in your future.

You are a conqueror in the making!

PERSONAL NOTES

Printed and bound by PG in the USA